LA RONDE

LA RONDE

A new adaptation by Max Gill
inspired by Schnitzler's classic

OBERON BOOKS
LONDON

WWW.OBERONBOOKS.COM

First published in 2017 by Oberon Books Ltd
521 Caledonian Road, London N7 9RH
Tel: +44 (0) 20 7607 3637 / Fax: +44 (0) 20 7607 3629
e-mail: info@oberonbooks.com
www.oberonbooks.com

A catalogue record for this book is available from the British
Library.

PB ISBN: 9781786821553
E ISBN: 9781786821560

Cover design by Mr. Will Stewart

Printed and bound by 4Edge Ltd, Essex, UK.
eBook conversion by CPI Group (UK) Ltd, Croydon, CR0 4YY.

Visit www.oberonbooks.com to read more about all our books
and to buy them. You will also find features, author interviews and
news of any author events, and you can sign up for e-newsletters
so that you're always first to hear about our new releases.

La Ronde was originally produced by Daniel Donskoy for Collaborative Artists Ltd in association with Heretic Productions.

It was first performed at The Bunker, London 11 February 2017.

Original Company
Leemore Marrett Jr.
Lauren Samuels
Alexander Vlahos
Amanda Wilkin

Creative Team

Director	Max Gill
Design	Frankie Bradshaw
Lighting	Jack Weir
Composition	Nathan Klein
Casting	Lucy Jenkins CDG
	& Sooki McShane CDG

Production Team

Producer	Daniel Donskoy
	for Collaborative Artists Ltd
Production Manager	Lucia Leyser
Stage Manager	Annabell Arndt

Sections marked with *** are filled with verbatim accounts

All characters can be played by either gender and pronouns in stage directions reflect this.

Each night the ten characters were assigned to the company of four actors at random by a wheel of fortune. Over three thousand different realisations of the play were possible.

'Can't have come cheap.'

'Nothing does.'

1

A brothel.

PROSTITUTE with a can of baked beans in their hands. Thai music plays.

BUS DRIVER stands on the other side of the room with their back to PROSTITUTE.

BUS DRIVER frustrated. Exhales. Fingers twitching. Deep breath.

PROSTITUTE: Are you ready?

BUS DRIVER: Do it.

  PROSTITUTE laughs.

  Beat.

  BUS DRIVER listens.

BUS DRIVER: Again. Do it again?

  PROSTITUTE laughs.

BUS DRIVER: Ignore what I said about Father Christmas. Is more like the Wicked Witch of the West but her balls have dropped.

  PROSTITUTE laughs.

BUS DRIVER: That's it. Fuck me you ain't half bad at this are you, love?

    Alright let's have it. Let's go from the top. I'm ready for you.

  They rush into position.

PROSTITUTE: 'Would you like more beans?'

BUS DRIVER:	It ain't gonna work if you don't do it Spanish, is it? How'd you forget you're fucking Spanish? Jesus wept. With a proper moustache and a daughter in a nunnery and all. Let's go back.
PROSTITUTE:	'Would you like more beans?'
BUS DRIVER:	Here we go.

BUS DRIVER gears them self up.

BUS DRIVER:	Come on. Get with it Mickey. Get with it. Alright. Ready now. Promise.

PROSTITUTE tips the can.

BUS DRIVER:	Wait! Hold up!
PROSTITUTE:	I did something wrong?
BUS DRIVER:	No. You're doing great. I'm just simmering and I just gotta wait for that rolling boil.

Beat.

BUS DRIVER:	Ready.
PROSTITUTE:	'Would you like more beans?'
BUS DRIVER:	Come closer and stand proper over me. That's it. I'll squat. I'm only six for God's sake. And I'm small for a six-year-old, let me tell you. And you're leerin'. That's it I wanna see your teeth. Alright. I got it. I'm holding the tray like this like butter wouldn't melt. You've got your rubber gloves on. That's it them rubber gloves like it was yesterday. Alright.
PROSTITUTE:	You ready?
BUS DRIVER:	Yes I'm fucking ready what's it look like come on.
PROSTITUTE:	'Would you like more beans?'
BUS DRIVER:	No I don't like beans. *(Nods.)*

PROSTITUTE pours beans on BUS DRIVER

BUS DRIVER: Laugh! Now!

PROSTITUTE laughs.

Pause.

BUS DRIVER: Got a tissue?

PROSTITUTE hands BUS DRIVER tissues.

BUS DRIVER wipes face. Throws tissue to the floor.

BUS DRIVER: Fuckin' hell. Fuckin' hell. Two hours we been here? I can't think of anything else. You're not helping me right if I'm perfectly honest.

PROSTITUTE: Don't think what you want. Feel with your body.

BUS DRIVER: Yeah yeah…No, no, no. 'Cos now I'm thinking about what I'm feeling, aren't I!

PROSTITUTE: I will do whatever you want.

BUS DRIVER: Then tell me what I want. You're the fucking expert. 'Scuse me. I forgot, you're a virgin that's right. This is your first time. Jesus. Tell me honest. Am I fucked up 'cos there's nothing wrong with me? Eh? Am I a blinking fucking weirdo because I don't wanna do it normal but I don't want a pineapple right up in my arse? Tell me. You must have seem some proper class A honey-nut-loopy-cunts in your time.

PROSTITUTE: Maybe you just need a relationship.

BUS DRIVER: Me? Jog on, love. A relationship? Do one. Happy Fucking Birthday; here's a little bear holding a great big heart, oh and look what's written on it in the prettiest little pink circle, 'From me to you, you to me. Roses are red, violets are blue, I love you, I actually have a thing for dead trout.' *(Laughs.)* Sorry, I get

9

	carried away me. I get carried away. Should see me on a Friday.
PROSTITUTE:	It's charming.
BUS DRIVER:	Are you lying to me?
PROSTITUTE:	Of course not.
BUS DRIVER:	'Cos I can tell when people are mugging me off. My grandmother was a medium and all. Says Jack the Ripper used to come for breakfast. It was that Eastern European bloke all along.
PROSTITUTE:	We only have ten minutes left.
BUS DRIVER:	Alright, alright who are you? The bleeding White Rabbit?!
PROSTITUTE:	We can give animals a go?
BUS DRIVER:	My mum bred Persian cats one summer.
PROSTITUTE:	And did they bite you?
BUS DRIVER:	They might have done. My mum couldn't shift them. Not a big market for Persians in Tottenham back then. Don't know what happened to them kittens come to think of it. Eyes like saucers. Probably ended up in my packed lunches.
PROSTITUTE:	*Miaow.*
BUS DRIVER:	Don't embarrass yourself. *(Beat.)*
	I feel like I'm… like a fucking cyst. Whatever's inside it's gotta come out and you know it's gonna be disgusting but you know it's gonna feel so good and you don't wanna look at it but you kinda want to eat it. I wanna want something, and fucking get it. You hear me? Have it and have it like proper good. Get over here. One last try. Bend down.

BUS DRIVER pushes PROSTITUTE over.

BUS DRIVER:	How's that feel? Nice?
PROSTITUTE:	Lovely.
BUS DRIVER:	What about there?
PROSTITUTE:	Lovely.
BUS DRIVER:	Good.
PROSTITUTE:	You ready?
BUS DRIVER:	Born ready.
PROSTITUTE:	What you gonna do to me?
BUS DRIVER:	Sex.
PROSTITUTE:	Yes! What kind of sex?
BUS DRIVER:	Sexy sex.
PROSTITUTE:	Do your worst.

Beat.

BUS DRIVER:	Maybe if I got to know you a bit better, I'd get there.
PROSTITUTE:	I can be whoever you want.
BUS DRIVER:	No. I want you to be you.
PROSTITUTE:	I'll do my best.
BUS DRIVER:	What was your name again?
PROSTITUTE:	Sunset.
BUS DRIVER:	How old are you then?
PROSTITUTE:	Nineteen.
BUS DRIVER:	Where's Sunset from? That's a nice name.
PROSTITUTE:	My parents.
BUS DRIVER:	Sunset's not your real name is it?
PROSTITUTE:	Nah.
BUS DRIVER:	What's your real name then?
PROSTITUTE:	Jazz.

BUS DRIVER:	Jazz? That's an interesting name.
PROSTITUTE:	I wanted to be a singer.
BUS DRIVER:	And why aren't you a singer now?
PROSTITUTE:	It's complicated.
BUS DRIVER:	Something proper tragic happened to you, didn't it?
PROSTITUTE:	It did.
BUS DRIVER:	Really bad. Like Dickens bad.
PROSTITUTE:	Worse.
BUS DRIVER:	But you don't want to talk about it.
PROSTITUTE:	Never.
BUS DRIVER:	Did Daddy touch you?
PROSTITUTE:	That's right.
BUS DRIVER:	And you took to drugs to blot out the pain. It's always the way.
PROSTITUTE:	But I don't do that no more.
BUS DRIVER:	And you like what you do. In fact, you love it.
PROSTITUTE:	I love it.
BUS DRIVER:	You like the human contact. You couldn't do it if you didn't enjoy it. That's what people don't get about your type; you're not like real people, you couldn't do it if you didn't enjoy it.

They fall onto the bed together. PROSTITUTE starts to undress.

BUS DRIVER:	I want you to be comfortable.
PROSTITUTE:	Don't worry about me.
BUS DRIVER:	I want you to have a good time.
PROSTITUTE:	I'm having the time of my life.
BUS DRIVER:	Does my breath smell?

PROSTITUTE: Like roses.

BUS DRIVER: If I'm paying you I want you to be proper *in* to it.

PROSTITUTE: There's no worry about that.

BUS DRIVER: So whatever yeah?

PROSTITUTE: Pure fucking filth.

BUS DRIVER: You'll do anything I want. Anything I want. That's right.

They roll about on the bed.

BUS DRIVER pulls away.

BUS DRIVER: Just give me a minute.

PROSTITUTE sits up and lights a cigarette.

Pause.

PROSTITUTE: You ever thought you might…?

BUS DRIVER: What?

PROSTITUTE: Be of another persuasion.

BUS DRIVER: Why d'you say that? What makes you think that?

PROSTITUTE: Most people like to dip in a toe. Give it a go.

BUS DRIVER: Well not me. Never have never will. Thank you very much. Disgusting. You got one of those for me?

PROSTITUTE gives BUS DRIVER a cigarette. Puts out their hand. BUS DRIVER gives them a few coins.

BUS DRIVER: Look. I'm sorry.

PROSTITUTE: Don't be.

BUS DRIVER: I'm letting you down and all. You wouldn't do this if you also didn't want a a bit of fun.

They sit and smoke in silence. PROSTITUTE twists a gold chain with a medallion around their neck.

BUS DRIVER: That can't have come cheap.

PROSTITUTE: Nothing does.

BUS DRIVER: I should still be at work.

Pause.

PROSTITUTE: You get fired?

BUS DRIVER: No.

PROSTITUTE: Sick?

BUS DRIVER: I killed someone.

PROSTITUTE stands.

BUS DRIVER: Not like that. I ain't gonna cut your throat so sit yourself back down. I knocked someone down. At noon on the dot. Drive the 149 see.

PROSTITUTE sits.

BUS DRIVER: Came from nowhere. Just by London Bridge. At the roundabout. Some posh prick comes through in a police convoy, big black car, I swerve to side. Person steps out. That's it.

PROSTITUTE: Maybe it was suicide.

BUS DRIVER: Come off it. What's wrong with a bottle of bleach down Poundland?

PROSTITUTE smokes.

BUS DRIVER: Poor sod. Roadkill in pinstripe. I don't know. But then they came and they strapped them all up anyway in one of them things that looks like you're blasting off into space. Thunderbirds are go. Thick black blanket comes out. I just wander about after. Head spinning like a fucking carousel. Hairs on my arm, right, they're like static. Feeling in my stomach like ink blotting. I wanted to touch someone. To feel skin. To feel red inside. Tried to have a wank, wasn't hitting that bullseye, you know. Looked online on one

of them applications, too much like fucking
hard work. I don't give two hoots that
your 'interests' are badminton and fucking
Bulgarian or something. Do you know what I
mean?

PROSTITUTE: Do you want me to lie like I've hit the
pavement?

BUS DRIVER: No. Thanks for the offer though. I can't get
their face out my head. Like goulash.

BUS DRIVER puts their head on PROSTITUTE's shoulder. Nestles.

Pause.

BUS DRIVER starts to kiss PROSTITUTE on their body. Up and down.

*BUS DRIVER leans in to kiss PROSTITUTE on the lips. PROSTITUTE
pushes BUS DRIVER away. BUS DRIVER kisses PROSTITUTE's neck.
Tries to kiss PROSTITUTE's lips.*

PROSTITUTE: I don't kiss. I told you.

BUS DRIVER: But I want a kiss. That's what I want.

PROSTITUTE: You can have *anything*.

BUS DRIVER: I want a kiss.

PROSTITUTE: I'm not kissing you.

BUS DRIVER: I'll have my dosh back then.

PROSTITUTE: No refunds.

BUS DRIVER: I'll give you more cash if that's all you're after.

PROSTITUTE: I don't kiss for nothing.

BUS DRIVER: That's the only thing I want.

PROSTITUTE: And you're not gonna get it.

BUS DRIVER: But I've paid you.

PROSTITUTE: Hands off.

BUS DRIVER: I ain't leaving till I get my kiss.

BUS DRIVER grabs PROSTITUTE and tries to kiss them. They scrabble on the bed.

Lights down.

* * *

Lights up.

PROSTITUTE and BUS DRIVER on the bed. BUS DRIVER tries to kiss PROSTITUTE on the lips.

BUS DRIVER: Come on. Just one. Just one kiss.

PROSTITUTE: *(Shouting.)* Help! Room 2!

BUS DRIVER jumps off PROSTITUTE.

BUS DRIVER: Why won't you kiss me? Eh? Something wrong with me eh? Not so great yourself. You're fucking dirt, you know that. Shit on my shoe.

PROSTITUTE takes out BUS DRIVER's money, shows it to BUS DRIVER, and throws it on the floor.

Beat.

BUS DRIVER scrabbles to pick up the cash.

PROSTITUTE leans in suddenly and kisses BUS DRIVER on the lips, for a moment.

BUS DRIVER takes their belongings and leaves the room. PROSTITUTE straightens the bed.

PROSTITUTE composes themselves.

The doorbell rings.

'*Quicken with kissing: had my lips that power,*

Thus would I wear them out.'

2

A small flat. Sound of traffic rumbling outside.

CLEANER smiles and laughs.

BUS DRIVER: This you then?

CLEANER: Thank you for really wonderful evening.

BUS DRIVER: Pleasure was mine yeah.

CLEANER: You want come in for drink? A night hat?

BUS DRIVER: Night-cap.

They enter CLEANER's flat.

CLEANER: I ask you to take shoes off.

BUS DRIVER: Oh, sorry, yeah.

CLEANER: I don't ask, I order. I am dictator! *Laughs.*

BUS DRIVER kicks off shoes.

CLEANER: You want slippers?

BUS DRIVER: I think I'm probably alright, thanks.

CLEANER: Put on slippers. Thank you for understanding.

BUS DRIVER puts on slippers reluctantly.

BUS DRIVER: Nice place.

CLEANER: Thank you.

BUS DRIVER: You live here alone? Just you?

CLEANER: I like to be independent.

Pause.

BUS DRIVER:	You got moola for the taxi? Shall we sort that out now?
CLEANER:	Moola?
BUS DRIVER:	Cash. Coin.
CLEANER:	Of course. How much?
BUS DRIVER:	I paid for the wine didn't I which was a bit less than the food. So if you give me about nine eighty six…
CLEANER:	Here.
BUS DRIVER:	Is good to be equal. Just sort it out now.
CLEANER:	Yes.
BUS DRIVER:	I don't like people to feel like they owe anyone nothing.

CLEANER counts up the money and gives it to BUS DRIVER.

BUS DRIVER:	Cheers.
CLEANER:	I take your coat?
BUS DRIVER:	I think I'll leave it on for…alright, cheers.
CLEANER:	It is nice coat.
BUS DRIVER:	Really? It was a gift, actually.

CLEANER takes coat.

CLEANER:	Sorry for smell. *(Laughs.)*
BUS DRIVER:	Can't smell nothing.
CLEANER:	I was cooking goulash this afternoon.
BUS DRIVER:	Oh yeah I smell it.
CLEANER:	You want some? I get you some.
BUS DRIVER:	I'm still stuffed full from them sticky ribs, thanks.
CLEANER:	Just little bit to try?

BUS DRIVER:	No. I don't want goulash.
CLEANER:	You sure? Is recipe from home.
BUS DRIVER:	I don't like goulash.
CLEANER:	Is winter. You need fuel.
BUS DRIVER:	Fine.
CLEANER:	I bring drinks. I have beer, but also have bottle of Bollinger was given as gift by family we could open?
BUS DRIVER:	What we celebrating?
CLEANER:	If you wait for reason, you never drink champagne.
BUS DRIVER:	If you insist. I'll give you a hand opening it.
CLEANER:	No. I manage.
BUS DRIVER:	You sure? I can give you a hand.
CLEANER:	Stay.

CLEANER goes off to fix drinks and goulash. BUS DRIVER looks about the flat.

BUS DRIVER:	How long you been here then?
CLEANER:	*(Off.)* Couple of month. Make some money, try to send extra back home. If I can.

CLEANER enters with a bottle, two glasses of champagne and a bowl of goulash.

CLEANER:	Cheers.
BUS DRIVER:	Cheers.

Silence. They drink.

BUS DRIVER:	Nice this.
CLEANER:	I love champagne.

Pause.

CLEANER:	You try goulash?

BUS DRIVER: Oh right. Yeah.

BUS DRIVER tries the goulash.

BUS DRIVER: Yeah. Lovely.

CLEANER: Is easy. Just beans.

BUS DRIVER puts down spoon.

CLEANER watches.

BUS DRIVER has another spoonful.

CLEANER: So Mickey. I remember it says on your profile you like travel.

BUS DRIVER: Yeah. You?

CLEANER: I love.

BUS DRIVER: Been Spain. Canaries. You been Spain?

CLEANER: No.

BUS DRIVER: Spain's nice.

CLEANER: Beaches.

BUS DRIVER: Sandy. Bit of sunshine.

CLEANER: I love sunshine.

BUS DRIVER: Get's a bit grey here in London all the time. Raining.

CLEANER: So much rain.

BUS DRIVER: So grey. You feel it in your bones. It's fallacious. That's the word.

CLEANER: Don't ask me. *(Laughs.)*

BUS DRIVER: Means nasty.

CLEANER: How you spell?

BUS DRIVER: Fuck knows.

Laugh. Pause.

CLEANER: You also tick you like music?

BUS DRIVER: Did I? Yeah I like music.

CLEANER: I put on some music?

BUS DRIVER: Yeah I could listen to some music.

CLEANER: What music do you like?

BUS DRIVER: Like? All music really.

CLEANER puts on Latin American music. CLEANER sways to the music.

CLEANER: I love this.

BUS DRIVER: Yeah. Not so much.

CLEANER: You don't like?

BUS DRIVER: It's nice.

CLEANER: I think I must have salsa in my blood.

BUS DRIVER bops awkwardly along to music.

The music plays.

CLEANER: You have to be at hospital tomorrow?

BUS DRIVER: Not tomorrow. Day after.

CLEANER: You work part time?

BUS DRIVER: They give surgeons a break. Rota.

CLEANER: Is very tiring.

BUS DRIVER: That's right. Long hours.

CLEANER: But you help people every day. Saving lives.

BUS DRIVER: Yeah. That's why we do it, you know? You in then?

CLEANER: In morning. Graduate. Very clever. Help me with English.

BUS DRIVER: I should think so. On your hands and knees like that.

CLEANER: Come dance.

BUS DRIVER: I don't do dancing.

CLEANER:	Everyone dance.
BUS DRIVER:	Not me.
CLEANER:	Is just moving your body.
BUS DRIVER:	Exactly.
CLEANER:	And follow your heart. What could be easier?

BUS DRIVER stands and dances awkwardly. CLEANER takes them by the hand and they sway together.

CLEANER:	Woo! That's it, baby. Spin!
BUS DRIVER:	Yeah…
CLEANER:	You know you first person I meet who actually looks like photo.
BUS DRIVER:	That a good thing?
CLEANER:	Yes, of course! Better to, how to say, prepare for worst! *(Laughs.)*

CLEANER leans in for a kiss but BUS DRIVER misses them as BUS DRIVER twirls on the spot. They sway next to each other.

BUS DRIVER:	Who's the kid in all the photos everywhere?
CLEANER:	Is my daughter.
BUS DRIVER:	A daughter? Your profile didn't say you had a daughter.
CLEANER:	This problem?
BUS DRIVER:	Not at all. Right. Yeah. She's beautiful.
CLEANER:	Is back home. She lives with my parents.
BUS DRIVER:	Right.
CLEANER:	I miss her.
BUS DRIVER:	You don't see…?
CLEANER:	No. They leave with someone else.

BUS DRIVER:	My old man ran off with someone when I was six. Some bloke actually. It's all got a bit heavy, hasn't it?
CLEANER:	Heavy?
BUS DRIVER:	Means serious. Bit of a mood killer.
CLEANER:	Who is killer?
BUS DRIVER:	Me! Shouldn't have let me in your home, should ya?
CLEANER:	Is joke?
BUS DRIVER:	'Course it is. But only last week there was the body of some bird found behind some bins in Southwark who's met up with some nutter. Now it's got all serious again.
CLEANER:	You want more champagne?
BUS DRIVER:	Go on then.

CLEANER pours more champagne.

BUS DRIVER:	Thanks.

BUS DRIVER necks it.

BUS DRIVER:	It's funny. When I said just now that I wasn't…you know what? Don't worry.
CLEANER:	Say.
BUS DRIVER:	At lunchtime… No. It don't matter.
CLEANER:	Say.
BUS DRIVER:	Save it for another time.
CLEANER:	What you want to say?
BUS DRIVER:	Nothing. Nothing. I had nothing to say.

Pause.

They drink.

CLEANER:	Do you believe in love?

BUS DRIVER:	Love? What do you mean?
CLEANER:	Have you been in love maybe?
BUS DRIVER:	Yeah. 'Course.
CLEANER:	How did you find it?
BUS DRIVER:	Yeah s'alright.
CLEANER:	I don't know it is good feeling one hundred percent.
BUS DRIVER:	No.
CLEANER:	In past they believe love get passed through eyes, and down into heart, like ghost.
BUS DRIVER:	No well I don't believe in love like that, no. I mean it's just chemicals and stuff right? Like a glass of champagne or pills or something.
CLEANER:	Why it not work for you?
BUS DRIVER:	We both wanted different things. They wanted things one way, and I wanted them the other.
CLEANER:	What did you want?
BUS DRIVER:	I dunno. I 'spose neither of us knew what we wanted 'cos if we did know we would of known it was the same thing for the other but we never knew that.
CLEANER:	Funny.
BUS DRIVER:	Yeah. Funny.
CLEANER:	So funny.

CLEANER kisses BUS DRIVER. CLEANER runs their hands down BUS DRIVER's back and they fall onto the sofa bed. Goulash knocked onto the floor.

CLEANER:	Why don't you stay round?
BUS DRIVER:	Yeah alright then.

They take each other's tops off.

BUS DRIVER:	What's that scar then?
CLEANER:	I don't want to talk about it.
BUS DRIVER:	Fair enough.
CLEANER:	What's that tattoo?
BUS DRIVER:	I don't want to talk about it.
CLEANER:	I like you, Mickey. You are special person.
BUS DRIVER:	Oh right, cheers, thanks.
CLEANER:	Is good here?
BUS DRIVER:	Yeah. Comfy sofa bed. DFS is it?
CLEANER:	I dunno.
BUS DRIVER:	Don't worry.
CLEANER:	No?
BUS DRIVER:	Good deals there. You like me then?
CLEANER:	Of course.
BUS DRIVER:	I like you too, Kris.

Lights down.

* * *

Lights up.

BUS DRIVER asleep. CLEANER wakes and sits up to look at BUS DRIVER. Strokes their hair. CLEANER climbs out of the bed and starts to fold their clothes, discarded across the floor. CLEANER rummages through BUS DRIVER's pockets. CLEANER finds BUS DRIVER's wallet. CLEANER opens up the wallet and looks through the cards.

BUS DRIVER:	What you doing?

CLEANER drops the wallet.

BUS DRIVER:	You rifling through my money? I know your type.
CLEANER:	I was just folding. It fall out.

BUS DRIVER:	Well get your mitts off. That's intrusive that is.
CLEANER:	Is this a game for you?
BUS DRIVER:	Eh?
CLEANER:	You are not surgeon, are you? You drive a bus.

Beat.

BUS DRIVER:	What makes you think that?
CLEANER:	I see your bus driver card.
BUS DRIVER:	Right. I thought I'd left that at home.
CLEANER:	Why you lie to me?
BUS DRIVER:	I wanted to impress you.
CLEANER:	You did.
BUS DRIVER:	I'm still the same person. What I would've said is no different is it?
CLEANER:	Maybe not to you.
BUS DRIVER:	Look love I'm clearly not a surgeon, so I'm gonna level with you; if you gonna fall for it, you probably don't deserve much better.
CLEANER:	You need to leave.
BUS DRIVER:	You're chucking me out? You were noshing me off only a minute ago.
CLEANER:	I wish I did not.
BUS DRIVER:	Whether I'm a tramp or a bleeding astronaut what you put in your mouth is gonna be much the same, I'm afraid.

BUS DRIVER stands to go, throwing on clothes.

CLEANER:	Just go.
BUS DRIVER:	It's not like I raped you or nothing. You still wanted to bang me even if it wasn't me how you thought I was.

BUS DRIVER gathers their things.

BUS DRIVER: Chances of a second date?

Silence.

BUS DRIVER: Not that I'm looking for anything serious.

CLEANER: Please. There is door.

CLEANER moves BUS DRIVER towards door.

BUS DRIVER: Can we keep in touch?

CLEANER: Goodnight.

BUS DRIVER: I'll send you a message online.

CLEANER: Go.

BUS DRIVER: Or I'll send you a letter once you've calmed down. Know where you live now.

BUS DRIVER leaves.

'The people who know that you will never be as
interesting as the people you pretend to be.'

3

STUDENT sat with open books. CLEANER clutching cleaning products.
Classical music on radio.

CLEANER:	*(Attempting but failing to say.)* Rural Juror.
STUDENT:	Rural Juror. Difficult to get your tongue around.
CLEANER:	*(Attempting but failing to say.)* Rural Juror.
STUDENT:	Ru-ral Ju-ror
CLEANER:	*(Attempting but failing to say.)* Rural Juror.
STUDENT:	The 'R''s more like a 'W'.
CLEANER:	William Wainwright was a Wurwal Juwor in Worce-ster-shire.
STUDENT:	These things take time. God's punishment after all. Tower of Babel. You may not have heard of it, of course.
CLEANER:	I did not know you are religious.
STUDENT:	I'm not religious, God no. I have an academic interest in religion. Particularly the Old Testament. I'm a Sadist, you see. I have a penchant for the esoteric.
CLEANER:	A what?
STUDENT:	A penchant.
CLEANER:	I thought it was *penchant,* no? Like in French. *Mais je ne suis pas l'experte.*

Beat.

STUDENT:	...*Non*. Where did you learn English? I mean, start to learn.
CLEANER:	I learn from radio. From television. Teacher in school sometimes teach me in break. But was very strict. Make mistake? *Wham.*
STUDENT:	They hit you?
CLEANER:	Yes, of course.
STUDENT:	Goodness.
CLEANER:	Different world.
STUDENT:	Yes. I dare say. Isn't it illegal?
CLEANER:	I don't know. Law isn't there to stop people, only catch them.
STUDENT:	I see.
CLEANER:	I think best way to learn a language is in love. Excuse me, George. Your feet.

CLEANER kneels down and cleans the floor around George's feet.

STUDENT:	You don't believe in love do you?
CLEANER:	Me? No, no. Do you George?
STUDENT:	Ha. Ooh, careful of my coat. Was a gift. Worth more than both of us.
CLEANER:	I'm sorry.
STUDENT:	Actually, Kris, could I ask you to find a time to do this room later on? My mind's rather spinning with ideas.
CLEANER:	I'm sorry, George. I distract you.
STUDENT:	It's only that I'm starting a very problematic paragraph on plosives in twelfth century Bulgarian.
CLEANER:	Is for degree?
STUDENT:	Doctorate. If you could leave now.
CLEANER:	I finish quick. In 'the blink of an eye.'

STUDENT: Good but go now. You're very distracting.

CLEANER: I go.

CLEANER leaves. STUDENT looks down at their books. STUDENT flicks through pages and attempts to write. Stops. Thinks.

STUDENT: Kris!

Pause. CLEANER reappears.

CLEANER: Yes, George.

STUDENT: Would you mind terribly getting me a glass of water?

CLEANER: Of course.

CLEANER disappears. STUDENT waits. CLEANER reappears with water.

STUDENT: Thank you so, so much. Superstar.

CLEANER: I go clean bathroom now.

STUDENT: No. Stay in here. And do the floor in here.

CLEANER: While you working?

STUDENT: While I'm working.

CLEANER gets on their hands and knees and starts to wipe the floor. STUDENT watches. STUDENT gets down on their hands and knees.

STUDENT: Let me help you there.

CLEANER: No. Is okay.

STUDENT: No, please. It must be murder for your back.

CLEANER: George, no.

STUDENT: I insist.

CLEANER: No. *I* insist. This is my job. This is what I am paid to do.

STUDENT stands.

STUDENT: Tell me what you're doing now.

CLEANER: I polish floor.

STUDENT:	And how does one polish a floor exactly?
CLEANER:	You take cloth and rub hard. Round in circle. Spray. Like this.

CLEANER demonstrates.

STUDENT:	Spray. Push. Rub. Rub. Push. Spray
CLEANER:	Over and over again.
STUDENT:	How much do I pay you an hour, Kris?
CLEANER:	6.50. Actually, George, you have not paid yet for last week.
STUDENT:	Haven't I? I'm so forgetful. It must be jolly difficult to live on that pay, what with travelling, cleaning products, and what not.
CLEANER:	The more you work the more you make.
STUDENT:	And Kris, tell me, do you tell people what you do?
CLEANER:	Yes. Is nothing to be ashamed.
STUDENT:	So you would tell friends, acquaintances, that you were my cleaner?
CLEANER:	I am your cleaner, yes.
STUDENT:	What did you dream of doing when you were a child?
CLEANER:	I don't know. Doctor maybe.

Beat.

STUDENT:	Who else do you clean for today?
CLEANER:	First I come here. Somedays I go to hotel. Then I go to house of writer to clean flat and look after cats.
STUDENT:	Good job? Good client? Is that what you call them? Makes it sound a bit sordid.
CLEANER:	Very dirty. Toilet, like battlefield.

STUDENT:	And does that make it better? Do you like to clean the dirt?
CLEANER:	The difference after makes me feel good, yes. Satisfying.
STUDENT:	Maybe I should make more of a mess here then.

Beat.

CLEANER:	Then sometimes I clean in school in canteen. This I don't like. Children disrespecting. They think because there is cleaner they have to make more mess.
STUDENT:	Did you get in lots of trouble when you were a child?
CLEANER:	I was a 'fallacious' child. Make fire in garden. I have scar. Sent to live with grandmother.
STUDENT:	I never got in trouble.
CLEANER:	You are Little Miss Perfect.
STUDENT:	My mummy was too busy making cocktails to notice. Then what?
CLEANER:	Seven thirty to nine I clean professor's house but I learn they in accident yesterday. House very tidy. Shame.
STUDENT:	So you make an average Tuesday…about sixty pounds. Long day. What if I were to pay you that just to clean mine? But only mine. Would you take it?
CLEANER:	Yes.
STUDENT:	Thank you Kris, that's everything I wanted to know. I'm going to need to get back to my work now.
CLEANER:	I go.

Kris leaves.

STUDENT waits.

STUDENT: Kris!

Kris reappears.

STUDENT: I do feel bad, Kris.

CLEANER: About what?

STUDENT: Me being in a position to pay you to do things I never want to do. Only because you need to.

CLEANER: I find pleasure in job.

STUDENT: I was wondering if you might be interested in earning a bit of extra pocket money then.

CLEANER: Always.

STUDENT: You don't know what it is yet. It might be something you have never done before.

CLEANER: I have done many things.

Beat.

STUDENT: I'm really rather struggling with my dissertation. And I find it much easier to process my thoughts when I hear them out loud.

CLEANER: I am opposite.

STUDENT: Well perhaps you should do a Phd then.

CLEANER: I don't know…

STUDENT: I wasn't being serious. I'd like for you to read out my notes. I will be scribe. It means I write as you speak. You must correct me if I make a mistake. That is very important.

CLEANER: If that is what you want.

STUDENT: It is. Think of it like a game. And I'll chuck you a couple of quid for every correct page.

CLEANER: Then I won't lose.

STUDENT: It suits you to be in charge.

STUDENT sits. Raises hands over keyboard of computer.

CLEANER: From the top of page.

CLEANER reads from notes.

CLEANER: 'Particularly in relation'

STUDENT types.

CLEANER nods.

CLEANER: 'To orthoepic norms and the use of certain morphosyntactic categories'

STUDENT hesitates.

CLEANER: 'To ortho-epic norms'?

STUDENT types.

CLEANER: You have missed the 'y' in 'morphosyntactic'.

STUDENT deletes.

STUDENT: From the top.

CLEANER: Do not make mistake again.

STUDENT: I won't.

CLEANER: Otherwise I will punish you.

STUDENT: Punish me?

CLEANER: Like in my village.

STUDENT: Like in your village.

CLEANER: You don't want that.

Beat.

STUDENT: Start again.

CLEANER: 'To orthoepic norms and the use of certain morphosyntactic categories'

STUDENT types.

CLEANER: 'However, it is proven that turbulence motivates high vocoid conditioned phonological stop assibilation…'

CLEANER stops. STUDENT waits. STUDENT rests hands on table.

STUDENT: Like in your village.

CLEANER strikes STUDENT across their hands with a ruler. STUDENT winces.

STUDENT: Keep going.

Beat.

CLEANER: 'Turbulence motivates'

CLEANER strikes STUDENT with the ruler.

CLEANER: 'motivates high vocoid conditioned phonological…'

CLEANER strikes STUDENT twice. CLEANER strikes them again.

CLEANER: 'Phonological'. Do not make mistake again.

STUDENT: I'm sorry.

CLEANER: Is that clear?

STUDENT: Very.

CLEANER: 'Stop assibilation.'

CLEANER strikes STUDENT.

CLEANER: I tell you not to make any mistake.

STUDENT types.

CLEANER: Again.

STUDENT types. Finishes.

CLEANER: Very good, I am almost impressed.

STUDENT turns to look at CLEANER. CLEANER pulls STUDENT in to kiss. CLEANER holds them back as their faces touch.

CLEANER: Not yet.

CLEANER throws papers at their feet.

CLEANER: Pick up.

STUDENT scuttles to pick up the papers around CLEANER. STUDENT kisses CLEANER up their calf but as STUDENT gets higher CLEANER pushes them back down to the floor.

STUDENT: I'll do anything you want.

CLEANER: Lick this floor clean.

STUDENT starts to lick the floor.

CLEANER: You are shit on my shoe. Cleaner. That's it. On your hands and knees.

CLEANER releases their foot from STUDENT. STUDENT rises and CLEANER takes them by the throat and pulls them in to kiss.

STUDENT: Let's do it. I'm ready. Break me.

STUDENT pushes CLEANER against the wall.

STUDENT: Rape and pillage me.

CLEANER: No.

STUDENT: Please.

CLEANER: No.

STUDENT: I'm begging you. I'll do anything.

CLEANER pulls STUDENT's hair.

STUDENT: Pull harder. Have me. Have me.

CLEANER takes a scarf and swings it in front of STUDENT. STUDENT gets on their hands and knees. CLEANER ties it around STUDENT's eyes.

CLEANER: Do not move a muscle.

STUDENT: Yes.

CLEANER: I said do not move a muscle.

STUDENT: I will do anything you say.

Lights down.

* * *

Lights up.

CLEANER releases STUDENT.

STUDENT:	You won't tell anyone about this, will you?
CLEANER:	I don't know.
STUDENT:	This is just our little secret, right?
CLEANER:	We haven't done anything wrong.
STUDENT:	No. Exactly.

CLEANER rearranges the room. STUDENT sits at their desk. They work in silence.

STUDENT:	I think you should start looking for other work, Kris. I think this will be our last session.
CLEANER:	I don't do good job?
STUDENT:	No, you do a very good job.

Beat.

CLEANER:	You want me to finish today?
STUDENT:	Please do. Then go.
CLEANER:	Then I will need money for this week and last.
STUDENT:	Aren't you interested to know why I don't want you to work for me anymore?
CLEANER:	No. I'm not.

Silence.

CLEANER and STUDENT continue their work.

'It makes you want to do something bad. You know?'
'Like what?'
'Like something really bad.'

4

A cheap hotel room. STUDENT and SPOUSE in each other's arms in bed.
Kissing. The sound of wind raging outside.

STUDENT: Jerry.

SPOUSE: Oh George.

STUDENT: Jerry.

SPOUSE: Yes, George.

STUDENT: This is heaven.

SPOUSE: George.

STUDENT: Oh Jerry.

SPOUSE: George.

STUDENT: Yes, Jerry

SPOUSE: This is heaven.

STUDENT: You know what I could never live without?
               The taste of your throat.

SPOUSE: How many times do you think we've done it?

STUDENT: I think I loved you before I even knew you.

SPOUSE: Yes that's it. Like that. Stop it. I don't deserve
               it. No don't stop it. I'm a monster.

   Lights down.

* * *

Lights up.

SPOUSE: George.

STUDENT: Oh Jerry.

SPOUSE: George.

STUDENT: Yes, Jerry.

SPOUSE: Imagine if I got caught. What are we doing?

STUDENT: Everything.

SPOUSE: You deserve an Oscar.

STUDENT: Why? What for?

SPOUSE: For playing the best fuck of my life.

Lights down.

* * *

Lights up.

They laugh. They kiss again.

SPOUSE: Let's try it like this.

STUDENT: Don't break me.

SPOUSE: How does that feel?

STUDENT: Beautiful. You're beautiful.

SPOUSE: I'm not beautiful. I'm hideous.

STUDENT: Don't say that.

SPOUSE: I'm so fucking hideous. How does that feel?

STUDENT: Perfect. You're perfect. Is that good for you?

SPOUSE: I don't want to know what's good for me.
Say it again.

STUDENT: You're perfect.

Lights down.

* * *

Lights up.

STUDENT: And the sunlight clasps the earth,

And the moonbeams kiss the sea;–

What are all these kissings worth,

If you kiss not me…Jerry.

SPOUSE: Did you write that for me?

STUDENT: Write it?

SPOUSE: I can't believe you wrote that for me.

STUDENT: Of course.

SPOUSE: I hate poetry.

STUDENT: It's not finished yet.

SPOUSE: I thought no one could save me. And then you walked into Babies & Badminton.

STUDENT: We're the lucky ones.

SPOUSE: Say my name.

Lights down.

* * *

Lights up.

STUDENT and SPOUSE lie next to each other.

STUDENT: Are you alright?

SPOUSE: Yes. Why do I not look alright?

STUDENT:	Are you sure? post coitum omne animalium triste est.
SPOUSE:	Whatever. Let's get some fruity cocktails sent up. Something with a bit of a twist.
STUDENT:	They're on me this time. I'd like to get them.
SPOUSE:	Go on then.
STUDENT:	Actually I don't have any cash.
SPOUSE:	Oh I know. Come here. Just a struggling, poor little student.
STUDENT:	Graduate.
SPOUSE:	You must be so tired from all that reading. Have a little snooze. Mummy will be right here when you wake up.

SPOUSE strokes STUDENT's head.

STUDENT:	Can we get dessert?
SPOUSE:	We'll get you an ice-cream.
STUDENT:	I don't like strawberry.
SPOUSE:	Alright. Mint chocolate then. Decadent and refreshing. Like us.

STUDENT snuggles into SPOUSE. SPOUSE picks up the hotel phone.

SPOUSE:	Oh, yes, hello there. Room 5. We've just closed our deal, and were wondering… sorry, could you put me through to someone who speaks English? Not to be demanding or anything. Jesus. Oh hello, yes, could we get a bottle of Bolli up to the room, we're celebrating an important business deal with a developing nation, and a large mint choc chip sundae. Thanking you. Bye now.
STUDENT:	Bolli?

SPOUSE: If we're gonna do it let's fucking do it. It's on me. Little treat. If only Charlie could see me now.

STUDENT: Would that be it?

SPOUSE: Don't say that. But no. Charlie needs me more. But I'd like, just for a minute, for us both to know. To see Charlie shrink a little. Deflate. Like a bus letting on a wheelchair. Just so it was known. And then I'd do a spell and Charlie would forget. But I'd know that just for one minute, we both knew.

STUDENT: Isn't Charlie suspicious where you've been?

SPOUSE: I really don't want to talk about Charlie.

Beat.

SPOUSE: Charlie could take Felix away from me.

STUDENT: Not your son. You're his full-time parent.

SPOUSE: Primary care giver.

STUDENT: But we could run away together.

SPOUSE: Where would we go?

STUDENT: Anywhere. Panama. Alaska. Mongolia.

SPOUSE: Oh my God. Let's do it. I'm serious.

STUDENT: Let's actually do it.

Beat.

SPOUSE: When you're married you'll understand.

STUDENT: You deserve to be treasured.

SPOUSE: No, I don't

STUDENT: You do.

SPOUSE: I do.

STUDENT: Like I do you.

SPOUSE: Like you do me.

STUDENT: Like a little fluffy Persian pussycat.

SPOUSE: Miaow.

STUDENT nibbles behind SPOUSE's ear.

SPOUSE: I'm wasted George. Squandered. I'm a peach
            you forgot was in the bottom of your bag
            until it's too late.

STUDENT: I bet Charlie doesn't love you like I do.

SPOUSE: Love?

Beat.

STUDENT: Love all the things there are to love about
            you.

SPOUSE: I know.

Beat.

STUDENT: Show me a picture of Charlie.

SPOUSE: No. That's not fair.

STUDENT: What does Charlie sound like?

SPOUSE: Sound like? I don't know.

STUDENT: Think.

SPOUSE: *Strong.*

STUDENT: What else?

SPOUSE: Um. Sounds s*mooth.*

STUDENT: And?

SPOUSE: *Decent.* Whatever./

STUDENT: /Interesting.

SPOUSE: /Or maybe *honest.*

STUDENT: Do you think Charlie sees anyone else?

SPOUSE: Charlie? No. Why?

STUDENT: Just wondering.

SPOUSE: Never. Charlie? As if. No. Charlie loves me too much.

STUDENT: And you?

SPOUSE: There's being in love and there's being in love and wanting to spend the rest of your life with someone.

STUDENT: Which one are you?

SPOUSE: Don't ask me.

Beat.

SPOUSE: Give me your phone.

STUDENT: Why?

SPOUSE: Just give it to me.

STUDENT hands over phone.

SPOUSE: I'm going to ring Charlie so you can hear.

STUDENT: Don't.

SPOUSE: I know.

STUDENT: No.

SPOUSE: I'm going to do it.

STUDENT: Don't do it. I don't want to hear.

SPOUSE: I am. Is that naughty?

STUDENT: You're going to do it?

SPOUSE: I am.

STUDENT: Do it then.

SPOUSE rings CHARLIE. Voicemail.

SPOUSE: 141…Voicemail… Must be seeing some patient.

SPOUSE hangs up.

STUDENT: Patient? You said Charlie worked in the city.

SPOUSE:	Works in St. Barts hospital, which is in the city of London, yes.
STUDENT:	As what?
SPOUSE:	Does it matter? Why does everyone always need to know what everyone does all the time? I used to work in charity. Just because Charlie's off saving lives doesn't mean that I'm any…

STUDENT's phone rings.

SPOUSE:	Who is it?
STUDENT:	I don't know.
SPOUSE:	Is it Charlie?
STUDENT:	I don't know.
SPOUSE:	Don't answer it.
STUDENT:	What if it's Charlie?
SPOUSE:	If you don't answer it will be more suspicious.
STUDENT:	Really?
SPOUSE:	Answer.

STUDENT answers.

STUDENT:	*(Different voice.)* Hello?
SPOUSE:	Who is it?
STUDENT:	Yes. I'm in a hotel at the moment. No I'm not alone.
SPOUSE:	Oh God. Don't say that.
STUDENT:	Oh my God.
SPOUSE:	Hang up!
STUDENT:	When? Who knows?
SPOUSE:	Who knows what?

STUDENT hangs up.

SPOUSE: Who was it?

STUDENT: Something's happened.

SPOUSE: What?

STUDENT: Bad news.

SPOUSE: What?

STUDENT: Something's happened to Vic.

SPOUSE: Oh thank God for that I thought it was
               Charlie. Who the fuck's Vic?

STUDENT: My professor.

SPOUSE: Of course. Yes.

STUDENT: We were going to the theatre tonight.

SPOUSE: Well that's good news, you can spend more
               time with me. Kiss.

STUDENT: A bus.

SPOUSE leans in.

STUDENT: No.

SPOUSE: Kiss.

STUDENT gets up.

SPOUSE: Where are you going?

STUDENT: I need to go.

SPOUSE: You're just going to leave me like that? Leave
               me here to stew like some dog outside the
               supermarket?

STUDENT: I really liked Vic.

SPOUSE: I didn't realise you were lovers.

STUDENT: We weren't.

SPOUSE: Don't try and make this all about you.

STUDENT: I'm not making this about me.

SPOUSE: What about me? I'm the one risking
               everything to be out here rutting you in a
               fucking Premier Inn. In Hillingdon.

STUDENT: I'll ring you.

SPOUSE: Don't bother. I'll be at home with Charlie.
               I'm married in case you forgot.

STUDENT: If that's what you you think is best.

SPOUSE: Of course it's not what I think is best. What a
               silly thing to say.

STUDENT picks up their bag.

SPOUSE: Ridiculous.

Pause.

SPOUSE: Charlie! George! Stay! I'm sorry. I'm so
               sorry. I said sorry!

STUDENT: Can I have some cash to get home?

SPOUSE: Stay for a little bit.

SPOUSE gives STUDENT money. They embrace. They kiss.

SPOUSE: I've got an idea.

STUDENT: What is it?

SPOUSE: I don't know if I can say. If I say, it might
               ruin it.

STUDENT: It's not an idea unless you can say it.

SPOUSE: Hurt me.

STUDENT: Yes.

SPOUSE: And pretend to be Charlie.

Beat.

SPOUSE: I knew you'd be shocked.

STUDENT: I'm not shocked.

SPOUSE: You'll do it?

STUDENT: No. I don't want to be Charlie.

SPOUSE: Can I piss on you?

STUDENT: Fine.

SPOUSE: But you won't be Charlie? Why not?

STUDENT: Because I'd be doing it out of love.

Beat.

STUDENT: And I don't think that's what you want, is it?

STUDENT gets up and leaves.

SPOUSE sits on the bed.

Pause.

Takes out their mobile phone.

SPOUSE: Hi darling, it's me. In Waitrose. Yes, don't
            worry. Much better. Do you want me to pick
            you up anything for dinner?

'And all happy at home?'
'Just lovely, thank you.'

5

Darkness. SPOUSE and DOCTOR in bed. On opposite sides of the bed.

A baby monitor gurgles. SPOUSE switches it off.

They sleep.

Silence.

Rustling. The sound of something under the covers. SPOUSE switches on a bedside lamp. DOCTOR, covers over their head, masturbates.

* * *

DOCTOR climaxes. SPOUSE pulls the cover from DOCTOR's head. DOCTOR opens their eyes.

DOCTOR rolls over to the other side of the bed and sleeps.

SPOUSE switches off the bedside lamp.

A baby monitor gurgles.

6

DOCTOR with papers at desk. Two cups of tea. DOCTOR puts papers down and exhales. DOCTOR stands and paces. A knock at the door.

DOCTOR: Come in.

    PROFESSOR enters, nervous.

PROFESSOR: Doctor Lupton, how are you? You look well.

DOCTOR: Thank you. And how are you Vic?

PROFESSOR: Do I not look well then? *(Laughs.)*

DOCTOR: You look just like you always have. How are things?

PROFESSOR: Oh God, I'm all over the place really. Having one of those days. Headless chicken alert. I'm supposed to be having people over for dinner tomorrow. Originally I said only six but then someone asks to bring their partner and all of a sudden it's fifteen and I don't know whether or not to do a standing buffet or cram everyone into my kitchen like Piccadilly Circus. God knows what I'm going to cook. Going round the bend. Cuckoo. Have you cooked for fifteen?

DOCTOR: A goulash or similar is easy just to leave on the hob. Before we start, can I take your coat?

PROFESSOR: I think I'll leave it on for…alright, thank you.

DOCTOR: Nice coat.

PROFESSOR: It was a gift, actually. Where would you like me? On the bed? Next to you?

DOCTOR: Come and sit next to me.

PROFESSOR: How's everything coming along here? When did I last see you? About three weeks wasn't it? Was it three weeks?

DOCTOR: Yes. About that.

PROFESSOR: How is your son?

DOCTOR: He's wonderful, thank you.

PROFESSOR: And all happy at home?

DOCTOR: Just lovely, thank you.

PROFESSOR: Jerry well?

DOCTOR: Very well. Playing a lot of badminton.

Pause.

DOCTOR: Can I offer you anything to drink? I've just made some tea.

PROFESSOR: No. I'm fine, thank you. That's what they give you when it's something bad isn't it. Sugary tea.

Beat.

DOCTOR: What is your understanding of why we did the MRI and biopsy?

PROFESSOR: To have a closer look at the pain around my spine.

DOCTOR: I do have some news to tell you. Bad news, unfortunately.

Beat.

PROFESSOR: Okay. Maybe I will have that tea.

Takes tea from desk.

DOCTOR: The results do indicate a cancer of the spinal tissue. Which means it has returned.

Beat.

DOCTOR: I was also hoping for a better result.

PROFESSOR: It's fine. It's fine.

PROFESSOR takes a sip of tea.

DOCTOR pushes a box of tissues to PROFESSOR.

DOCTOR: This must be very difficult for you.

DOCTOR puts their arm on PROFESSOR.

PROFESSOR: Embarrassed. I feel embarrassed. That's what I feel. I've just started renovating the upstairs bathroom, new students, one graduate I thought I actually might quite fancy. Meant to be going to see *Antony and Cleopatra* tonight. *(Laughs and knocks over tea.)* Oh, sorry. I'm so sorry. Let me clean that up.

DOCTOR: Sit down

PROFESSOR: I thought you said you got it all last time?

DOCTOR: What I should have said was we got everything we could see.

PROFESSOR: Righto. Okay.

DOCTOR: Is there anyone you'd like to call?

PROFESSOR: No. Not just yet.

DOCTOR: Have you got any family nearby?

PROFESSOR: Not that I've spoken to for a little while. But I will. Now.

DOCTOR: Do you have any questions?

PROFESSOR: What happens next?

DOCTOR: Do you want to know everything? I can instead outline a pain treatment plan?

PROFESSOR: It's like that is it?

DOCTOR: There isn't anything more we can do for you here.

PROFESSOR: So where else is there?

Pause.

PROFESSOR: I see. That's clear enough.

DOCTOR: I know this must be difficult for you.

PROFESSOR: And for you as well. Everyday. Do you get training?

DOCTOR: Yes.

PROFESSOR: Awful. Not you. You're doing a brilliant job.

DOCTOR: Thank you.

PROFESSOR: You know the waiting for bad news is worse than actually getting it I think.

DOCTOR: I understand.

PROFESSOR: Do I get to see you again?

DOCTOR: I will refer you to my colleague. But you can come and see me as much as you like.

PROFESSOR: Do you have a timeline then?

DOCTOR: Every patient is different. It is difficult to say.

PROFESSOR: Years? Months?

DOCTOR: More likely the latter.

PROFESSOR: That's all I want to know.

Pause.

DOCTOR: Do you have any questions for me?

PROFESSOR: Yes. Lots. But I don't know if you can answer them.

DOCTOR: When you get home write any questions you have on a piece of paper and send them to me. Don't look online. I am not abandoning you and I will make sure that you won't suffer in pain.

PROFESSOR: Now's the time to enjoy making plans, I suppose. Do that thing.

DOCTOR: There is often a comfort in that.

PROFESSOR: Can I hug you? Is that allowed? In your training?

DOCTOR: Of course you may.

PROFESSOR throws themselves on DOCTOR and the tears come. DOCTOR strokes their back.

DOCTOR: You take as long as you need.

PROFESSOR: You must have other patients to see?

DOCTOR: You take as long as you need.

PROFESSOR: When I was better, I actually missed seeing you. Isn't that ridiculous?

Beat. PROFESSOR holds them tight.

PROFESSOR: Fuck it. Fuck it. Fuck it. Fuck it. Oh that feels good. You know when you're sat on the bus and you try to plan your own funeral? It's the music I can't do. Still, you can't be embarrassed or awkward when you're dead, that's some solace. I don't want to be maggot's meat but I don't like the idea of being blasted so unceremoniously in an oven like a clay pot. And there's no way you get all your ashes out the other end. Probably just an elbow or something. Or worse. I read about this couple in Ancient Egypt who were found buried together. It was two men. Royal manicurists. They think they're the first historical example of a gay couple. Can't remember their names.

DOCTOR: I would concentrate on living.

PROFESSOR: I've never been much good at that either.

DOCTOR tries to pull away. PROFESSOR holds them tight.

PROFESSOR: Please, stay like that.

DOCTOR: If it's any comfort that was some of the hardest news I've given. My mother. When she was not much older than you. That's why I do what I do. You actually have the same birthday.

Pause.

DOCTOR: Is there any more I can help you with today?

PROFESSOR: I have had more pain in my side. Would you have a look?

DOCTOR: Certainly.

PROFESSOR takes off their top. They stand with their arms out.

DOCTOR: Whereabouts is the pain?

PROFESSOR: Just around my kidneys I think.

DOCTOR feels their side.

DOCTOR: How is that? Tender?

PROFESSOR: A bit.

PROFESSOR leans back into DOCTOR. PROFESSOR takes DOCTOR's arms and wraps them around their body.

PROFESSOR kisses DOCTOR on the cheek. DOCTOR waits. DOCTOR kisses PROFESSOR on the cheek.

Lights down.

* * *

Lights up.

PROFESSOR dresses by the bed. DOCTOR at their desk.

DOCTOR: Someone will be in touch with you soon, via telephone.

PROFESSOR: Have you done that before, Doctor?

DOCTOR: No. I haven't. And I think I probably shouldn't again.

PROFESSOR: I understand. You might lose your job.

DOCTOR: There's that.

PROFESSOR: Is it wrong?

DOCTOR: It's unprofessional.

PROFESSOR: No. I mean me. Isn't it wrong to desire me?

DOCTOR: It's natural.

PROFESSOR: Is it?

DOCTOR: We felt something, didn't we?

PROFESSOR: I'll send you that piece of paper. With the questions.

DOCTOR: Here's a prescription. For the pain.

Hands prescription.

PROFESSOR: Bye Dr. Lupton.

'I've got an idea.'

'What is it?'

'I don't know if I can say. If I say, it might ruin it.'

7

PROFESSOR and SCREENWRITER drink tea in SCREENWRITER's kitchen. Gregorian chant playing.

PROFESSOR: Still full of crap?

SCREENWRITER: Started to clear out the attic. All the toys are still there. Plays I wrote as a child. Even the headless body of my doll, remember that?

PROFESSOR: God I was such a shit. I don't know why anyone put up with me.

SCREENWRITER: Well they didn't really. They sent you to boarding school and gave me the en-suite.

PROFESSOR: You know you might just undo five years of therapy, thank you very much. And how is he then? Dad.

SCREENWRITER: Good. Fine. Strange. Almost like he can choose when to zone in and out of knowing what the hell is going on or not.

PROFESSOR: That's hardly a change.

SCREENWRITER: Carer's sweet. Dim. But sweet. Must be about nineteen. Lots of make-up. Almost *this* thick off her face. I don't know why you want to look like Dolly Parton while you're putting in a catheter but I think Dad's happy.

PROFESSOR: I'm going to go and see him soon.

SCREENWRITER: You should. As his mind rots, you see the man inside. And he's not very nice. He's a piece of work. It's refreshing.

PROFESSOR: When is it going to get really bad?

SCREENWRITER: Difficult to say. Doctor says every patient's different.

PROFESSOR: I mean when nappies and setting fire to yourself starts.

SCREENWRITER: Six months? What's worrying is that his blood pressure and cholesterol are that of a thirty-year-old apparently. He'll probably outlive us all.

PROFESSOR: Typical. We'll have to work out a visit rota when the shit hits the fan. Actually.

SCREENWRITER: Are you sure you don't want anything to eat? We've got something in a pot left over from last night. Kris made it.

PROFESSOR: Nothing sweet?

SCREENWRITER: If you'd only given me some warning.

PROFESSOR: Sorry for steaming in here like this. I'm so happy to see you.

SCREENWRITER: And you.

PROFESSOR: Where are the cats?

SCREENWRITER: Out. They find Gregorian chants wearisome.

PROFESSOR: You seen Alex at all?

SCREENWRITER: Fuck no. Apart from on the side of every bus.

PROFESSOR: I did see *The Southwark Strangler*. It was rather good, actually.

SCREENWRITER: I pitched them the idea. Years back.

PROFESSOR: Alex was really rather good, too. Plays a narcissistic blood sucking call girl killer rather well.

SCREENWRITER: Surprise.

PROFESSOR: Don't fancy *Antony and Cleopatra?* I'm off tonight.

SCREENWRITER: We don't speak to each other.

PROFESSOR: Never say never.

SCREENWRITER: Never.

PROFESSOR: Not to pry. And how is the writing coming along?

SCREENWRITER: Yes. Yes. Good. Got a potential commission at some various places. Thinking of the months ahead. Lots of ideas. Yeah. Good.

PROFESSOR: I'm so glad. I'm so happy to see you.

SCREENWRITER: Yes, you keep saying that.

PROFESSOR: Well, it's true.

PROFESSOR takes SCREENWRITER's hand and squeezes it.

PROFESSOR: I'm sort of over it all. You know?

SCREENWRITER: Over what?

PROFESSOR: Kind of everything. I was sad but that's boring for everyone, including me. My sadness bores me.

SCREENWRITER: I know what you mean.

PROFESSOR: Whoever I'm with always ends up being the worst person I could possibly ever have chosen. Eventually. Which only makes it worse that it takes me so long to realise. Every time. Fascist or socialist, all our friends without exception are ghastly, self-seeking, almond-croissant-guzzling, Cath Kidston cunts. Work's shit, always has, always will be.

SCREENWRITER: It's all about finding the glamour and fun in isolation and depression.

PROFESSOR: I mean we could move to Tuscany and have a cabbage patch and donkeys but we'd get bored.

SCREENWRITER: Provence isn't Provence anymore. N'est-ce pas?

PROFESSOR: It makes you want to do something bad. You know?

SCREENWRITER: Like what?

PROFESSOR: Like something really bad.

SCREENWRITER: Like… stealing a wheel of brie on the self scanner at Waitrose?

PROFESSOR: No. Much worse. Like burn a school down. Just to really feel alive. Go to a children's party and kick the birthday girl. Push someone in front of a tube. Smash through that sweaty clingfilm boundary that tells us what we should and shouldn't do. Because playing by the rules doesn't make you happy, does it? Well, it doesn't make you not unhappy, which it bloody well should.

SCREENWRITER: In rush hour I stand against the wall not because I'm scared someone will push *me*.

PROFESSOR: Exactly.

Beat.

PROFESSOR: I've been AWOL and I'm sorry. I needed to get completely lost in order to get back to the start, you know?

SCREENWRITER: You don't need to apologise.

PROFESSOR embraces SCREENWRITER.

PROFESSOR: I've really missed you.

SCREENWRITER: I've missed you too.

PROFESSOR: At this rate you're the only cert at my funeral.

SCREENWRITER: Oh shut up. But I'll be there. With bells on.

They laugh into each other's shoulders. PROFESSOR pulls back and their faces are very close. PROFESSOR kisses SCREENWRITER. Almost on the mouth. They sit back from one another. Silence.

SCREENWRITER: That was nearly something bad.

PROFESSOR: Was it?

Beat.

SCREENWRITER: What shall we do about Dad's car?

PROFESSOR: The Fiesta?

SCREENWRITER: Still got some life in it.

PROFESSOR: Scrap it.

Beat.

PROFESSOR leans back in and kisses SCREENWRITER on the lips. They both laugh, quietly.

PROFESSOR: Do you remember that holiday in Spain?

SCREENWRITER: Locked in the annexe.

PROFESSOR: But this is different.

Lights down.

* * *

Lights up.

SCREENWRITER: I've got to prepare for a script meeting with a producer later and then I've got a talk at the British Library. I need to get ready.

PROFESSOR: Oh what's the talk on?

SCREENWRITER: Oh Genghis Khan and Mongolian sexual mores or something.

PROFESSOR: Epic.

SCREENWRITER: That was the right decision, wasn't it? Not to.

PROFESSOR: I think so, yes.

SCREENWRITER: We wouldn't be helping ourselves, or anyone really.

PROFESSOR: Quite right. I'll get out of your hair. I'll get a cab.

SCREENWRITER: I can call one.

PROFESSOR: I need to talk to you about something.

SCREENWRITER: I appreciate that but I really think it best we left it in its own box, in its place. Wherever that might be.

PROFESSOR: I'm stage 4.

SCREENWRITER: What?

PROFESSOR: I'm T4 N3 M1b or something, I don't know. It's come back.

SCREENWRITER: Vic, why didn't you say?

PROFESSOR: I've just been to the hospital. I came straight here.

SCREENWRITER: And?

PROFESSOR: It's not good.

SCREENWRITER: What do you mean?

PROFESSOR: It's not good news. Curtains. Kaput. Fin.

Both stand frozen.

They make to embrace each other.

Stop themselves.

They embrace. Relief.

SCREENWRITER: We're here for you.

PROFESSOR: Shut up.

SCREENWRITER: Well, I am.

PROFESSOR: Well, I won't be for you.

SCREENWRITER: You don't know that.

PROFESSOR: Yes but medicine does.

SCREENWRITER: I might go first. You just don't know.

PROFESSOR: I don't know if I should tell Dad. Don't tell him. Promise me.

SCREENWRITER: I don't know if he'd really register.

PROFESSOR: There's no point distressing him.

SCREENWRITER: For the next thirty years of his life.

They hold each other tight.

PROFESSOR: I don't want to tell anyone, I don't think. So you're the only person who knows, ok?

SCREENWRITER: I'm the only person.

PROFESSOR: Our secret. And then I think I'll just get a whole fuckload of smack or something and have it large. Jump in front of a bus or something.

SCREENWRITER: Why you?

PROFESSOR: Why not?

Lights.

'You won't tell anyone about this, will you?'
'I don't know.'
'This is just our little secret, right?'

8

SCREENWRITER stands in a lift. ACTOR enters the lift. SCREENWRITER looks at the floor. ACTOR stares at their phone. ACTOR looks round, sees SCREENWRITER, and tries to leave the lift. The doors close before ACTOR leaves.

The stand in silence, tapping feet.

The lift breaks down.

They wait.

SCREENWRITER: Oh dear.

ACTOR: You gonna press the fucking button or what?!

SCREENWRITER: Nice to see you too, Alex.

ACTOR: You know what? Fuck you.

    ACTOR presses the button.

ACTOR: Hello? Hello there? Is anyone there? We're stuck in the fucking lift. Get us out of this fucking lift. Jesus Christ I'm going to have a meltdown. I'm claustrophobic.

SCREENWRITER: Deep breaths.

ACTOR: You stay out of this. I'm claustrophobic. You know that. I bet you organised this. I don't wanna even *look* at you.

SCREENWRITER: Might struggle for the time being.

ACTOR: I've missed your fucking wisecracks so much. So much. *(Presses button.)* You know what? No sweat. We've got the fucking comedy roadshow up here so we're just great. Fucking asshole.

ACTOR takes a pill.

Presses button again.

ACTOR: Excuse me? I refuse to die in your shitty lift. Do you want Alex Gold to suffocate in your shitty lift? It's Alex Gold.

No response.

SCREENWRITER: And the crowds go wild.

ACTOR: I actually don't know how this even could get any worse. Literally.

SCREENWRITER: Lift plummets to the floor. We both die.

ACTOR: Shut up.

SCREENWRITER: Wrapped in each other's arms.

ACTOR: You're a fucking sick fuck.

SCREENWRITER: Get out of my life.

Pause.

ACTOR: How much air is there in these fucking things? My chest feels tight.

SCREENWRITER: I saw you in *The Southwark Strangler.*

ACTOR: Oh you did? You a stalker now too or what?

SCREENWRITER: You made some brave choices. The Alex Gold everyone used to love.

ACTOR: Before you tore up my psyche, pulled down your pants and shitted on my shattered selfdom. *(Closes eyes.)* 'Hiranmayena Pathrena, Sathyasyapi Hitham Mukham'

SCREENWRITER: Funny.

ACTOR: 'Hitham Mukham…' What?

SCREENWRITER: No. Nothing.

ACTOR: 'Thatvam Phooshanna…'

SCREENWRITER: How nowadays people go so far to discover the person they are only to refuse the person they find.

ACTOR: 'Thatvam Phooshanna…' I'm sorry were you speaking to me? I have equipped myself to see you as the person you are. An aggressor, Toni. And a baby. And a people pleaser. And a passive aggressor. And a negator. And an enabler.

ACTOR gets out a cigarette. SCREENWRITER watches as ACTOR struggles to light it.

ACTOR: Are you just gonna stand there?!

SCREENWRITER proffers a lighter. ACTOR smokes.

ACTOR: I'm so over this. I am so over this. What the fuck are you even doing here anyway?

SCREENWRITER: Script meeting.

ACTOR: I'm meeting a major, major director. I'm late because the roads were shut off because of some weirdo under a fucking bus.

SCREENWRITER: To think we might never have met.

ACTOR: What's the script about then? Your shrivelled genitalia? Is there a part for me in it? Where I go back and cut it all off?

SCREENWRITER: I don't know yet. I've had writer's block.

ACTOR: Myself and the citizens of this great nation are so saddened to hear that.

SCREENWRITER: I'm seeking help. I will get there.

ACTOR: No, you won't. You'll never heal. Psychiatry is a barrage of shitty reason shouting at shittier madness from the other side of the shitty pitch. In fucking thunder and lightning. One just ain't gonna hear the other.

SCREENWRITER: Grateful for your support, as ever.

ACTOR: I mean, didn't I give you enough material for at least one decent short?

SCREENWRITER: I've already made your career once as it is.

ACTOR: I turned lead into gold in that movie.

SCREENWRITER: At least people pay me to be me, not someone else.

ACTOR: Except they don't really pay you, do they?

SCREENWRITER: You're merely a vessel for other people's minds.

ACTOR: And bodily fluids. I cheated on you. A lot. Write about that.

SCREENWRITER: Let's not go down that road again.

ACTOR: Oh we're gonna go down there. And it's a well-trodden-yellow-brick-fucking-dirt-track. Remember the Japanese Olympic swimmers? How do you think I got that 5* review? Mark Billingsley and a strap-on. Pretty much the entire company of *Swan Lake*...

SCREENWRITER: I'm not going to call you a slut if that's what you want.

ACTOR: I even screwed Vic. In the ass.

SCREENWRITER: Vic?

ACTOR: Pretty shitty, huh? Pretty shitty.

SCREENWRITER: Why Vic?

ACTOR: Because Vic was always yours, and I wanted to fuck what was yours. Obviously.

Beat.

ACTOR: Yeah? That hurt didn't it? That hurt real good.

SCREENWRITER: I planted the drugs in your bag at Heathrow.

Beat.

ACTOR: I'm sorry?

SCREENWRITER: I put them in. Just before security.

ACTOR: And you…? And you watched me…?

SCREENWRITER: Handcuffed.

ACTOR: I knew it.

SCREENWRITER: I watched you strut in to court in your black shades and your little black suit. Looking perfectly repentant and perfectly devilish. Just like I watched you in your first showcase.

ACTOR: And watched me sob in the stand. My hand on the Bible.

ACTOR does sign of the cross.

SCREENWRITER: And held your hand on the tarmac and waved you off to Nevada. To stop you.

ACTOR: But you weren't there to hold my hand when I was sitting on the toilet, shitting and vomming and pissing and scratching myself raw so desperate for a hit…

SCREENWRITER: '…It feels like I'm a cyst ready to burst.' We all read the article. So moving.

ACTOR lashes out at SCREENWRITER. They grapple.

ACTOR: Eat my shit.

SCREENWRITER: You destroy everything you touch. You're a poison. A blight. I thought you wanted me because you loved me but I know now it was only because you hate yourself.

ACTOR: You wanna know why?

SCREENWRITER: Because you won't let yourself trust anything.

ACTOR: I can't.

SCREENWRITER: Except chemicals to pump round your own squalid self.

ACTOR: Because how the fuck else am I supposed to know who or what is *real* otherwise? Except for me. Except for what *I* feel. Do you know hard it is to have fucking love and care and attention and obsession flung at you like rotten tomatoes?

SCREENWRITER: Then stop mutilating those that really try to love *you*, not Alex Gold, *you*. The people who know that you will never be as interesting as the people you pretend to be.

ACTOR: They're the only people I can control.

SCREENWRITER: And you choose to eviscerate them. To hurt them.

ACTOR: I know I never hurt you because I know you never feel.

SCREENWRITER: Wow.

ACTOR: 'Proust this, Plato that'. I am not some dusty fucking barrel of other people's cerebral diarrhoea, like you. I am energy. I feel. I own my patch, and I am responsible for the topiary and watering of my patch. But unfortunately, my patch is affected by energies like you. Bad energies. Like a mosquito. Buzzing around. Bzzzzzz. Not even a mosquito. A slug. You're a slug sitting there, eating all the lettuce in everyone's patch just because you have a hunger to *deconstruct* but you know what? Soon there's not gonna be any lettuce anymore, for anyone. You are tragic. You have all these notions in your head that are never going to amount to anything. You, your body, you're immaterial. And when you are finally dead you will leave no trace.

SCREENWRITER pushes ACTOR against the wall. They struggle.

ACTOR: Get off me.

SCREENWRITER: You get off me.

ACTOR: Help! Rape!

SCREENWRITER: I'm going to destroy you.

ACTOR: I will gut you like a fish.

They hold each other's wrists and wrestle.

As their heads touch they give way to a passionate kiss.

Lights down.

* * *

Lights up.

SCREENWRITER and ACTOR, spent.

The lift moves.

They jump up to dress.

ACTOR: We must have woken it up or something.

SCREENWRITER: You really are a slut.

ACTOR: Thank you.

SCREENWRITER: I hope the show goes well tonight.

ACTOR: I still fucking despise you.

SCREENWRITER: You too. But at least it means we can be honest with each other.

ACTOR: That might be the first not moronic thing you've ever said.

SCREENWRITER: Thank you.

ACTOR: I've got a date with their Royal Highness tonight. Thought you might like to know.

SCREENWRITER: Just don't be yourself.

Ding.

SCREENWRITER: This is me.

ACTOR: Good luck with the script. Ciao.

'*Is this a game for you?*'

'*Eh?*'

'*You are not surgeon, are you?*'

9

Dressing room. ACTOR still as Cleopatra. ROYAL in their arms, script in hand, enacting a scene from the play. Sound of theatre tannoy.

ACTOR: Quicken with kissing: had my lips that power,
Thus would I wear them out.

ROYAL: I am dying, Egypt, dying:
Give me some wine, and let me speak a little.

ACTOR: No, let me speak; and let me rail so high,
That the false housewife Fortune break her wheel,
Provoked by my offence.

ROYAL: The miserable change now at my end
Lament nor sorrow at; but please your thoughts
In feeding them with those my former fortunes
Wherein I lived, the greatest prince o' the world,
The noblest; and do now not basely die,
Now my spirit is going; I can no more.

ACTOR: Noblest of men, woo't die?
Hast thou no care of me? shall I abide
In this dull world, which in thy absence is
No better than a sty? O, see, my women,

ACTOR nudges ROYAL.

71

…And die….

The crown o' the earth doth melt. My lord!
And there is nothing left remarkable
Beneath the visiting moon.

ROYAL kisses ACTOR. They fall into a romantic pose.

ROYAL: Oh Cleopatra.

ACTOR: My King.

Lights down

* * *

Lights up.

They are still in exactly the same romantic pose.

ROYAL: *You* are my queen tonight, and I, your most
                humble servant. No crown. No sceptre. Just
                flesh.

ACTOR: Me? The pock-marked and grease-painted
                whore.

ROYAL: You, to me, are the sun behind the
                mountains, a smile on a newborn's lips,
                the purr of a sleeping cat. You are beauty
                because when I see you I need to know
                more. An Islamic ceiling, an oriental fabric.
                Irrelevant, minute details that blossom into a
                turbulent heaven.

ACTOR touches ROYAL.

ACTOR: Are you ready to see the face of God with
                me?

ROYAL: But I do already. And you do in me. We walk
                into a room and there is fearfulness but the
                people are not afraid. We are blessed with an
                image not connected to these acne-riddled
                vessels. We are fantasy; art, history, glory.

ACTOR:	But don't you crave me? Don't you crave my love?
ROYAL:	Love is hideous. Love can have no beauty because it seeks beauty.
ACTOR:	But is there not beauty in that hope?
ROYAL:	Hope is lack. Inadequate. Inferior. A hole.
ACTOR:	Should we not try to fill that hole?
ROYAL:	For what? When you have, what will you see? Yourself? Better to disappear in the torture of impossible delight.

ROYAL stands.

And with that, my Queen, I must leave you.

ACTOR:	But Your Highness, when will I see you again?
ROYAL:	Must we see each other again?
ACTOR:	To know me.
ROYAL:	We knew each other before we had even met. Good night.
ACTOR:	Wait.

ROYAL leaves.

ACTOR stands still.

ACTOR pulls off their golden robe and lets it fall to the floor.

73

'I can be whoever you want.'

'No. I want you to be you.'

'I'll do my best.'

10

Thai music plays.

ROYAL and PROSTITUTE in bed together.

The lights do not go down.

ROYAL withdraws and dresses.

PROSTITUTE:	I've seen you before, haven't I?
ROYAL:	Wouldn't think so.
PROSTITUTE:	No. I swear I don't forget a face. You famous or something?
ROYAL:	Me? No. Not at all.
PROSTITUTE:	What do you do then?
ROYAL:	I drive a bus.
PROSTITUTE:	Take your word for it.

ROYAL takes out a gold necklace.

ROYAL throws it to PROSTITUTE.

ROYAL:	Here, take this.
PROSTITUTE:	Can't have come cheap…
ROYAL:	Nothing does.

ROYAL leaves.

PROSTITUTE puts the chain round their neck. Bites the gold.

The doorbell rings.

End.

WWW.OBERONBOOKS.COM